Counting Lions

By Adeline Zubek

Gareth Stevens
Publishing

Please visit our website, www.garethstevens.com. For a free color catalog of all our high-quality books, call toll free 1-800-542-2595 or fax 1-877-542-2596.

Library of Congress Cataloging-in-Publication Data

Zubek, Adeline.
Counting lions / Adeline Zubek.
    p. cm.— (Animal math)
Includes index.
ISBN 978-1-4339-5664-5 (pbk.)
ISBN 978-1-4339-5665-2 (6-pack)
ISBN 978-1-4339-5662-1 (lib. bdg.)
1. Counting—Juvenile literature. 2. Lion—Juvenile literature. I. Title.
QA113.Z825 2011
513.2'11—dc22

                                        2010048166

First Edition

Published in 2012 by
Gareth Stevens Publishing
111 East 14th Street, Suite 349
New York, NY 10003

Copyright © 2012 Gareth Stevens Publishing

Designer: Haley W. Harasymiw
Editor: Therese M. Shea

Photo credits: Cover, pp. 1, 5, 7, 9, 11, 12, 13, 15, 17, 19, 20, 21 Shutterstock.com.

Printed in the United States of America

CPSIA compliance information: Batch #CS11GS: For further information contact Gareth Stevens, New York, New York at 1-800-542-2595.

Contents

Boldface words appear in the glossary.

Big Cats

Lions are big cats. Most lions live in Africa.

How many lions do you count?

A lion has short fur. It has long hair on the end of its tail.

How many lions do you count?

7

Boy lions grow hair around their neck. This hair is called a **mane**.

How many manes do you count?

Girl lions are smaller than boy lions. A girl lion is called a **lioness**.

How many lionesses do you count?

Prides

Lions live in groups called **prides**.

Which of these prides
has 5 lions?

Families

Baby lions are called **cubs**. They have spots on their fur.

Does this picture show 2 or 3 cubs?

Lion families stay together for about 3 years.

How many lions do you count in this family?

17

A Lion's Life

Lions like to hunt animals at night.

How many lions do you count?
How many zebras?

Lions spend most of their day sleeping.

How many sleeping lions are in each picture? How many altogether?

Glossary

cub: a young lion

lioness: a girl lion

mane: hair around the neck of an animal

pride: a group of lions

Answer Key

page 4:
1 lion

page 6:
2 lions

page 8:
3 manes

page 10:
2 lionesses

page 12:
page 13 pride

page 14:
2 cubs

page 16:
4 lions

page 18:
2 lions, 1 zebra

page 20:
1 lion, 3 lions,
4 lions altogether

For More Information

Books

Joubert, Beverly, and Dereck Joubert. *Face to Face with Lions*. Washington, DC: National Geographic, 2008.

Tourville, Amanda Doering. *Lions Leaving: Counting from 10 to 1*. Edina, MN: Magic Wagon, 2009.

Websites

Great Cats

nationalzoo.si.edu/Animals/GreatCats/catskids.cfm
Read about lions and other big cats. Solve puzzles using their pictures.

Lions

kids.nationalgeographic.com/kids/animals/creaturefeature/lion/
See more photos of lions and watch videos of them in action.

Index